by **John C. Crystal**
and **Richard N. Bolles**

Where Do I Go From Here
With My Life?

*A very systematic, practical and effective life/work planning manual
for students, instructors, counselors, career seekers and career changers*

A Continuum Book / The Seabury Press · New York

Library of Congress Cataloging In Publication Data:

Crystal, John C.
  Where do I go from here with my life?

  (A Continuum book)
  1. Vocational guidance.   2. Applications for
positions.   I. Bolles, Richard Nelson, joint author.
II. Title.
HF5381.B63513   331.7'02   74-8188
ISBN 0-8164-9234-4

The Seabury Press
815 Second Avenue
New York, N.Y. 10017

Copyright © 1974 by Richard N. Bolles and John C. Crystal,
Crystal Management Services, Inc.
Printed in the United States of America

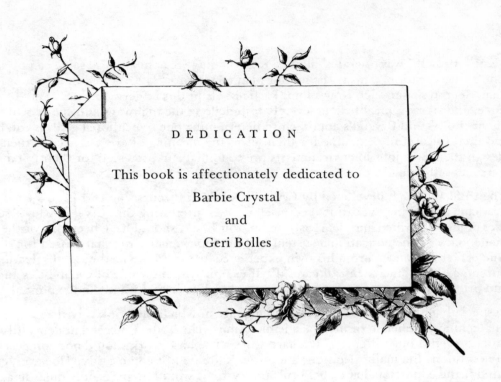

DEDICATION

This book is affectionately dedicated to

Barbie Crystal

and

Geri Bolles

FOREWORD

"Know thyself" was Socrates' dictum for attaining wisdom and the same can be said for choosing and finding one's true vocation. This is the master plan of the process described in this book, and it is no less arduous than Socrates' approach to wisdom. Participants in this undertaking are likely to find their education, experience, and stereotypical beliefs severely tested along the highways and byways over which the authors take them. Bolles and Crystal's approach to determining one's vocational goals is total. Not only are the participants required to carefully examine for themselves the meaning of every aspect of their experience, but to literally design their own jobs in environments preexamined and pretested for their potential to provide opportunity for personal self-actualization.

The total approach developed by Crystal over the last fourteen years is now emerging in various forms among academically trained vocational counselors. It is interesting that Crystal, who is self-trained apparently by the techniques described and demonstrated in this book, should have been one of the first to do something about the inadequacy of the educational system and the superficiality of what passed for vocational counseling to provide true career guidance. From his own experience he must have learned that selecting a satisfying career is not the outcome of gimmickry but of careful self-examination not only of capabilities and knowledges but of values and priorities. A satisfying career is invented and built, not found and exploited.

I especially enjoyed the simple, direct language in which the book is written. It is remarkably free of cant and the technical gibberish of most academic tomes. The writers succeed in demystifying the vocational guidance process even though it emerges as hard work. The hard work should not come as a surprise since under the best of conditions the major decisions about one's life do not come easily. However, career decisions could be facilitated if the educational and socio-cultural systems would prepare individuals in a systematic manner for career choice. This these systems do not do, and hence, individuals seeking to make a rational choice must do all the work all at once.

I differ with the authors in one respect. I believe that only the most exceptional persons could go through this process by themselves, and that it wouldn't be desirable even if they could. Experiencing decision making in the company of others seems to me an essential part of the process. Nevertheless, I recommend this book heartily to all helpers of those seeking career guidance.

Sidney A. Fine
The W. E. Upjohn Institute for Employment Research
Washington, D.C.

Contents

We sincerely hope that this manual will serve as a source of help and encouragement to many people to help themselves to analyze their capabilities, accomplishments, and interests and to constructively plan for their future career and their life. Although initially conceived as a help for IEEE members, we now realize the processes and concepts described in this manual should be beneficial to other engineers, scientists, and individuals of whatever field who will have the opportunity or necessity to move from one job or career to another as their life needs change, as well as to students in colleges or even high schools.

What gave IEEE its interest in this subject? The extensive unemployment of engineers and scientists in the aerospace and defense electronics fields starting in 1969-70 triggered a number of questions and requests of the IEEE and other engineering societies regarding what they were doing to provide help to their members in their search for new jobs. In addition to the immediate problems associated with enabling its members to get reemployed, members of the IEEE Washington Section in particular felt that it was desirable that the IEEE should provide an on-going service to its members in career-guidance and career planning. In providing such a service for its members, the IEEE could help prepare engineers so that inevitable termination of projects would not be so abrupt a disturbance to their lives and plans. Ironically, successful performance on major projects by engineers, scientists, and planners tends to hasten the day when the project will be complete, and the participants' services will no longer be needed for that project. The Apollo trips to the moon are a case at point.

The idea of the IEEE meeting this need by holding Seminars based on the most effective system available was suggested by Washington IEEE members to provide immediate help to some engineers but more importantly to train others to be able to help many more IEEE members to better consider and plan their future. Under the able chairmanship of Bob Bishop, their Continuing Education Committee conducted a study of the entire career planning field and discovered that the process desired was already being taught in McLean, Virginia. The appropriate arrangements were made with the designer/developer/teacher of this process and help was sought from H.E.W. to support such a seminar. This manual is an outgrowth of the seminar that was held with joint H.E.W., State of Maryland, and IEEE sponsorship. IEEE is grateful for this H.E.W. and Maryland support and wishes to thank the responsible people for this encouragement.

The IEEE is pleased to have been a catalyst in bringing together the people involved in making this book possible. In particular, I wish to thank IEEE member Bob Bishop for his enthusiasm and unstinting efforts in making all this happen. Without him, this manual would not exist at this time. In addition, I earnestly hope that many thousands of IEEE members and others will be able to live a fuller, richer, more complete life as a result of the guidance that they receive from this manual for the planning of their career and of their life.

HAROLD CHESTNUT, PRESIDENT 1973
INSTITUTE OF ELECTRICAL & ELECTRONICS ENGINEERS
MARCH 5, 1974

The history of this manual

Anyone who would like to help job-hunters must begin by recognizing a very simple truth: altogether too many workers in America today, or people about to enter the job-market, do not really want *any* process that will help them make occupational decisions. Because, as one of the Harvard Studies in Career Development discovered, most workers do not see themselves as rational decision-makers, when it comes to their work. By the way they tell the stories of their life, they convey the undeniable feeling that they have no real freedom of choice when it comes to occupational decisions. They seem to choose their occupation absent-mindedly, and they picture such occupational decisions as they subsequently made in a random, haphazard fashion—without any consciousness that there ever were real alternatives or possibilities set before them, from which—perforce—they were to choose.

The single factor which seems to influence people's career or occupation more than any other, is their first job opportunity into which they glide or slide, without much conscious decision or examination. This first job opportunity then conditions the whole subsequent course of their progress in the world of work, in altogether too many cases. It decrees what their degree of specialization shall be. It decrees their life-style. It decrees their attitude toward the whole world of work, and the readiness with which they greet—or abhor—personal change.

Much has been written, of course, about worker dissatisfaction, most notably the W. E. Upjohn Institute for Employment Research's own *Work in America* (prepared for the Department of Health, Education and Welfare), and *Where Have All the Robots Gone?* by Upjohn's Harold Sheppard, and Neil Herrick. These document what we instinctively know: how many people are mired in a rut, dedicated to a routine that they find completely frustrating, which yet they follow year after year—waiting perhaps for some kind of massive systemic change which will alter this unhappy state of affairs for them. Which is to say, they still rely on external factors to improve their occupational fate, rather than asking how they themselves can seize the moment and improve their own lot. They still do not see themselves as decision-makers, vis-a-vis their own occupational future.

The 'personnel experts', unhappily, tend to recommend the same kinds of solutions: systemic ones, which a massively apathetic System is able to produce only in a few privileged spots. Notwithstanding, think-tank after think-tank approaches problems of worker dissatisfaction, or mid-career change, with systemic biases, assuming that it is up to this institution or that to come up with solutions for the problem.

There are, however, bright spots upon the horizon. A larger and larger number of people are increasingly seeing themselves as occupational decision-makers, and asking for help in making occupational decisions—as evidenced by the increasing number of courses in 'career and life planning' that are being taught in colleges, in communities, in churches, professional societies, prisons and the like. As evidenced, also, by the growing number of professional societies which are interested, as IEEE is, in helping their people with occupational assessment and decision-making at mid-career.

All to the good. But the problem is: granted this interest, what kind of help can we give them? Who has developed some helpful and new ideas? And who has put together any comprehensive system for aiding occupational decision-making?

There are, to be sure, tools and aids which are already well-known, and of immense help to occupational decision-making. Typology kinds of framework can be very useful in giving somebody a quick fix on whither he or she is going. Of these, John L. Holland's *Making Vocational Choices: a theory of careers* (Prentice-Hall, Inc., 1973) is incomparably the best and most helpful.

But typologies do not always do justice, even in the best of hands, to the uniqueness of a particular individual. So, the $64,000 question has been: if a worker, or someone about to enter the job-market, had more time, and wanted to undergo some comprehensive, systematic process for surfacing his or her uniqueness, and then making practical occupational decisions on the basis of that uniqueness, what would that system or course look like?

In 1969, Richard N. Bolles was commissioned by his employer, United Ministries in Higher Education (a coalition of ten major Protestant denominations) to research such systems, in both the public and the private sector, to discover the most comprehensive system for aiding those who wanted help with their occupational decision-making. The subsequent research required two years and sixty thousand miles of travels. It was guided by four criteria:

(1) Does a particular decision-making system see itself as starting with what the worker or job-hunter wants; rather than what the employer wants?

(2) Does a particular system try to teach the student how to go about occupational decision-making and job-hunting as often as s/he may need to, for the rest of his or her life; rather than merely rendering services that rescue him or her for the time being, only?

(3) Does a particular system remain universal, helping all ages and kinds of people, with a good degree of expertise; rather than becoming elitist, helping only a privileged few?

(4) Do the counselors of a particular system know precisely how to go about the job-hunt, what works and what doesn't work; rather than innocently sending job-hunters out to step on the same old landmines that are hidden in the traditional job-hunting methods?

Auditing various systems, interviewing their clients afterward, Bolles' ultimate conclusion was that John Crystal of McLean, Virginia, had evolved a system which—while it had affinities, in various parts, with other systems, had synergistically evolved beyond any of them and was the most comprehensive, systematic and effective process to aid people with occupational decision-making and job-hunting, that exists in the country today.

The result of all of Bolles' research was published in *What Color Is Your Parachute: a practical manual for job-hunters and career-changers* (1972, Ten Speed Press, Box 4310, Berkeley, CA 94704).

THE HISTORY OF THIS MANUAL

Other agencies' investigations came to similar conclusions. Crystal was commissioned to conduct a pilot project for the Department of State, and subsequently for the Institute of Electrical and Electronics Engineers (Washington Section) in conjunction with the Maryland State Department of Education.

In sum, then, while many workers want no help with occupational decision-making and others want only some brief sort of process at best, there is a growing demand for such a comprehensive systematic process as this, for surfacing a person's uniqueness.

Consequently it has become evident that an instructor's manual *must* be produced for this process—something that, in his fifteen years as designer, implementer and practitioner of this process, Crystal has never had time to do. IEEE (Washington Section) fortuitously decided such a manual was an essential component of the Career Development program to which it was committing itself, and the State of Maryland contracted to have it written and tested. United Ministries in Higher Education released Bolles to work with Crystal on this project. The result is this combination training manual and classroom curriculum guide.

ACKNOWLEDGMENTS

The authors would like to express their profound gratitude to Dr. Ben S. Stephansky, Associate Director of the W. E. Upjohn Institute for Employment Research, in Washington, D.C., for his gracious offering of their facilities to the authors; to Sidney A. Fine and Harold L. Sheppard, of the Staff at the Upjohn Institute, for their helpful suggestions and encouragement; to James L. Reid, Assistant State Superintendent, and Elwood F. Adams, Supervisor, Manpower Development and Training, Maryland State Department of Education, for having the vision to support this innovation in occupational decision-making; to Dr. Howard A. Matthews, Director, and Thomas R. Hill, Education Specialist, of the Division of Manpower Development and Training, U. S. Office of Education, for their encouragement and support; to Mr. Samuel King, Chief, External Placement at the State Department, for his continuous cooperation and helpfulness; to Dr. Verlyn L. Barker, President of United Ministries in Higher Education, for his generous contribution of his staff (Bolles) to this project; and last, but hardly least, to Robert B. Bishop, Jr., Chairman, Continuing Education, IEEE (Washington Section)—without whose unswerving pursuit of excellency, and determination to overcome obstacles that would have made lesser men crumble, this project would never have happened.

JOHN C. CRYSTAL
RICHARD N. BOLLES

Instructions for using this manual.

This manual is designed so that it can be used four different ways:

I. By trainers of instructors or counselors, in career and life planning, occupational decision-making, and the job-hunt.

II. By instructors working with groups of students, of any age.

III. By instructors working with individuals, of any age.

IV. By self-motivated individuals working on their own, without an instructor.

We will explain what is required, in each case, and how the manual is to be used:

I. By trainers of instructors or counselors.

REQUIREMENTS: As a trainer, you should first have taken this course yourself, from start to finish, completing it in every detail. Hopefully, you will have been trained as an instructor in the process developed by the authors.* (Contact John C. Crystal, 6825 Redmond Drive, McLean, Virginia 22101 for information.) One of the standards, thereafter, is that evaluation cards are to be passed out to all would-be instructors subsequently trained by you, at the end of their training course. These cards are returned to John Crystal, and used to upgrade your expertise, through creative further training based on feedback.

HOW THE MANUAL IS TO BE USED:

The entire manual is explained in detail by the trainer, with heavy emphasis upon the column entitled "Group Techniques." But all columns are dealt with, in detail, in orientation sessions and mock-teaching practice exercises. Each trainee will need a copy of this manual.

II. By instructors working with groups of individuals.

REQUIREMENTS: As an instructor working with groups, you should first have taken this course yourself, from start to finish, completing it in every detail. You should have been trained as an instructor, then, in the process by the authors.* One of the requirements, thereafter, is that evaluation sheets be regularly used by you at the

---

* *While we are trying to protect individual students from inept instruction, no one recognizes the folly of accreditation programs more than we do; and therefore we are always open to the recognition of instructors or trainers with an inborn talent in this field; provided the evaluation cards are used regularly.*

end of your work with each group. These sheets are to be returned directly by the students to John Crystal, and are used to upgrade your expertise, through creative further training based on this feedback.

HOW THE MANUAL IS TO BE USED WITH GROUPS:

A. Before you meet with the group for the first time:

1. Familiarize yourself with the entire manual, by reading what is—for an instructor with groups—the 'command column', namely, the last one on each of the facing pages, entitled GROUP techniques. All the other columns are integrated to this fourth column.

2. We automatically assume you have already taken the course yourself, and therefore are completely familiar with the other columns. IF you haven't, they should be dealt with in this fashion: as you read the 'command column', you will note it is divided into sixteen sessions. *As you finish the directions for one of those sessions, interrupt your reading of this 'command column', and go read the appropriate supporting material in the other columns for that particular lesson or session—in the following order,* please, each time:
(a)   Student Program Element
(b)   Adjacent margins: Goals, and Errors
(c)   Appendices (if any)
(d)   The Counselor's column

B. The course can be taught in the following ways:

1. *Best:* Sixteen sessions, of three hours duration each, meeting every other week; except that three weeks should elapse between the first session and the second.
2. *Pretty Good:* Sixteen sessions, of three hours duration each time, meeting every week; except that three weeks should elapse between the first session and the second, and two weeks between the ninth and tenth.
3. *Good:* Sixteen sessions, of three hours each week—which may be divided into two weekly sessions (as in a school), one of two hours duration and one for one hour—or two weekly sessions of 1½ hours each, or three weekly sessions of one hour each, with no classes meeting during the second, third and fourth weeks.
4. *Bad:* Sixteen sessions, weekly or bi-weekly, which meet only for two hours or less in any given week. Experience has proved this leaves the students floundering, particularly the slower ones.
5. *Very Bad:* Not leaving any interval between the first and second sessions, or between the ninth and tenth. The consequence, experience has proved, is that the class becomes polarized between those who have kept up (anyway, often by working overtime at it) and those who are not able to keep up. Should this happen, the only way to rescue the situation is to divide the class in two, once polarization occurs, and allow the faster to proceed at their pace, while the slower go back over the material at their own pace a second time.

C. If you have any communication with the group before the first session, advise each student to purchase:
   1. A three-ring notebook.
   2. At least 300 sheets of 8½ x 11" three-holed paper—unlined, if the student will be typing his or her exercises; lined, if they intend to write the exercises longhand.
   3. Carbon paper.
   4. A number of file folders (12 to 24).
   5. File cards, 3 x 5", approximately 300.
   6. A paperback copy of *What Color Is Your Parachute?* (the essential student text). Ten Speed Press, Box 4310, Berkeley CA 94704.
   7. If it is an older group of students, ask them to bring their spouses with them to the first session.

D. Before the first session, you yourself as instructor will need to procure newsprint (big sheets, 24 x 36" if possible) from your local art supply store, paper outlet, etc. Also some magic markers (washable ink) from your art supply store or five & ten. This paper will be
   1. for you to put key words upon, when you teach or give orientation;
   2. for you to write questions, prior to small-group discussions, that the small groups are to consider;
   3. for the small-groups to use, during their discussion and in making report-back to the larger group.

E. It will be absolutely necessary for each student to have a copy of this manual/workbook, needless to say.

F. In constructing your class session curriculum, you do not need to use all the elements suggested, nor do you need to cover them in precisely the order indicated in the GROUP techniques column. Their order there is the systematic order for your own orientation, rather than the creative order for teaching, necessarily— though in some cases it may be (as is occasionally spelled out).

G. You will note that the form of address used in the STUDENT program element column and all the other columns (except the 'command column' for the instructor) is "You". This is to encoursge you in the use of this address form, always, in class. "You" is the nearest form in English to that which is, in other languages, the immediate, loving, and personal form of address. All other forms of address tend to show fear of people. So, in class, the instructor is encouraged to say, not, "Students will find that" etc., but "You will find that..."

H. You will note that the PROGRAM ELEMENT: INSTRUCTIONS TO THE STUDENT column is divided into two parts, depending upon whether the ELEMENT deals with identifying "What" the student wants to do, or "Where", or Both. This means that on most program pages, there is a blank column. Some instructors will wish to leave this blank; in other cases, you may wish to use the blank column to enter your own observations and bright ideas, to aid you in teaching this course.

III. By counselors working with individuals, of any age.

REQUIREMENTS: As outlined under "II. Instructors working with groups"

HOW THE MANUAL IS TO BE USED:

A. Disregard the final column on each page, entitled INSTRUCTOR. Go over the material, at the individual's own pace. Convey to him/her some of the purpose listed under Goals, some of the rationale listed on the appropriate Appendix pages whenever they appear, and some or all of the material under Error, and under Counselor. However, do not insult the intelligence of your individual student with over-kill, once you see that s/he has grasped your point thoroughly.

B. Each student *must* have his or her own copy of this workbook.

C. Cover the rest of the material in the appropriate Appendices at the appropriate time.

D. There are particular moments where your intervention will be necessary in almost all cases, and this is with skill-identification, and clustering. Few if any students are able to see all of their skills, without the point of view of a second party. Likewise with clustering.

E. You ought to ask the student to turn in, to you, a carbon copy of all the exercises which s/he does—particularly of the work-autobiography, since you will need this later when you are working with him/her on finding skill-identifications that s/he missed. This turning in of assignments also gives the student some measuring of how far s/he has come, in the course.

F. In going over the individual's assignment, you may want to use a yellow mark-over 'marker' (such as students commonly use in school) to 'overline' significant accomplishments, etc. to which you (or your student) may wish to return later on, in other exercises. This saves you from having to read the same material all over again two or more times. You only need re-read the material you have high-lighted.

IV. By self-motivated individuals, working on their own.

REQUIREMENTS: We know, from experience gathered over some fifteen years, that there is virtually no-one who cannot profit from this course when working hand-in-glove with a trained instructor. But if you have no instructor, and are trying to use this manual and follow this process all by yourself, there are certain qualities which you ought to possess. If you do not, you may find this process 'sticky' at least, and 'impossible' at worst. Those qualities are: some self-motivation and drive; some verbal ability to express yourself clearly; some ability to analyze things, and see sub-components; some ability to synthesize, or put things together in larger combinations; a decent memory of your past history; some awareness of your own feelings and dreams; curiosity and the willingness to investigate things, places and people; and some orientation toward achievement.

If you have hope, casting modesty aside, that you possess these qualities in even moderate amount, and there simply is no instructor for you to rely on and work with, then you may profitably try using this manual on your own. However, if that does not work for you, do not assume (please) that this process does not have any helpfulness for you. It only means that you must then go find an instructor.

HOW THE MANUAL IS TO BE USED BY AN INDIVIDUAL WITHOUT ANY COUNSELOR

- Disregard the column entitled INSTRUCTOR.
- Read everything else.
- Follow instructions unwaveringly.
- If you are having too much difficulty with one element, have someone else read the instructions to you. It may be that you are not hearing all of the instructions, for some reason. The 'eye-gate' is sometimes skilled at missing something, which the 'ear-gate' will then pick up.

CONCLUSION

IN ALL CASES, EACH STUDENT IS TO PURCHASE THE MATERIALS LISTED UNDER "How The Manual Is To Be Used With Groups, part C"—and is to keep all his or her homework exercises in that notebook.

If s/he is meeting with an instructor, individually or in group, the notebook (and all the exercises completed to date) are to be brought to that meeting, every time.

Before beginning this course it is important for you to have read INSTRUCTIONS FOR USING THIS MANUAL on page xiii.

The principal columns on each set of pages are the STUDENT'S columns—with the material there appearing in the first column if it deals with *What*, the second column if it deals with *Where*, and both columns if it deals with *What and Where* at the same time. Blank spaces on each page may be used for resting the eyes, for jotting down notes, reactions, etc.

The margins on either side of the STUDENT'S columns comment on the material in the STUDENT'S columns, the left hand margin commenting on Goals, and the right hand margin commenting on Errors to be avoided. Turn a few pages ahead to see what we mean. The COUNSELOR'S column on each right hand page is most commonly commentary on the Errors to be avoided, but may cover a wider range.

This Workbook is designed only to be used in conjunction with *What Color Is Your Parachute: A Practical Manual for Job-Hunters and Career-Changers* (Ten Speed Press, Box 4310, Berkeley, CA 94704, $4.95 paper) and every student must have his or her copy of that text, as well as of this manual.

student

THE PROGRAM ELEMENTS IN THIS FIRST
COLUMN HELP THE STUDENT IDENTIFY HIS/HER
PRIMARY **FUNCTIONAL GOAL** (WHAT)

THE PROGRAM ELEMENTS IN THIS SECOND
COLUMN HELP THE STUDENT IDENTIFY HIS/HER
PRIMARY **ORGANIZATIONAL GOAL** (WHERE)

counselor

instructor

1. Your Work-Autobiography

Include mates in the very first session, and encourage husband and wife to make this a joint project. Otherwise, just because this course is a whole life-changing process, it tends to leave the mate awfully far behind. Ideally, both husband and wife ought to write their separate work-autobiographies; but at the very least, they ought to work together on that belonging to the person taking this course.

High school or college students, taking this course, should be encouraged to adopt a pairing-off system with someone else (if possible, someone else who is meaningful to them)—in order to aid each other in putting the autobiography together.

The first class session should be a get-acquainted session, plus the presentation of the homework (the work-autobiography); accordingly, it might go like this:

FIRST CLASS SESSION
SOME SUGGESTED PROGRAM ELEMENTS

1. *Getting acquainted.* Each individual member of the class introducing him-/or herself to the rest of the class: who they are, where they came from, one significant fact about themselves.

2. *Expectations.* Breaking up into small groups of five to eight (no more) people in each group, to discuss the question: "What I hope to get from this course." Have someone in each small group appointed as convener (mover, leader, or whatever) and someone as "scribe". The answers of each to the topic prescribed, should be written on a sheet of *newsprint* (or any large piece of paper, procurable from your local art supply store, or the five & ten). Time for these small groups: 10—45 minutes. Then have a report-back to the total group when reassembled: each scribe putting up his/her newsprint sheet in the front of the room, and discussing it. Time devoted to the report-back: 10—20 minutes.

3. *Course background.* Give some background to what this course is all about, either in lecture form (most commonly) or in audio-visual form, if you are skilled in constructing your own audio-visuals. Basic material

First Class Session

student

By way of introduction to this course, please begin by reading Appendix A, page 169.

1. Your Work-Autobiography

Goal:
To encourage you to compile the basic material or goldmine, out of which you will then be able to extract those talents or skills which you have displayed and used throughout your life to date, no matter what your age.

Goal:
To be sure you compile enough material for you to mine.

We are asking you, first of all, to write a detailed work-autobiography of all your adult working experience starting with your first full-time job, or your graduation (whichever came first) and continuing through your present position.

It should be typed, and doublespaced, on 8½x11" paper, with one inch margins; or, if a typewriter is not available, handwritten in legible long-hand.

A copy (carbon or xerox) must be kept of *everything* in this course, including this.

Depending on the length of your life to date, it probably should end up being 50—200 pages, in length.

Be as specific as your records and memory permit.

Start the farthest back in history that you can, and work forward toward today.

The error to be avoided at all costs: Trying to give this work-autobiography 'just a lick and a promise'; giving it short shrift. Doing just an outline instead of in great detail. Writing only five to twenty-five pages.

counselor

READ THE THIRD COLUMN ON EACH PAGE
WHEN WORKING WITH **INDIVIDUALS**

instructor

READ THE FOURTH COLUMN ON EACH PAGE
WHEN WORKING WITH **GROUPS**, WORKSHOPS, CONFERENCES, ETC.

for this presentation: the first three chapters of *What Color Is Your Parachute?* and Appendix A, called "Introduction: An Overview of This Course".

4. *Questions.* Let the students ask any questions they may have, either *during* the above presentation, or (preferably) at its conclusion. If they ask questions to which you do not know the answer, respond honestly, "I don't know the answer, but I will find out for you." or "We will find out together, as time goes on."

5. *A simple overview of the homework* they are going to be asked to do: The Work-Autobiography.

1. Your Work-Autobiography

EXPERIENCE. You are sharing with the student a format that has been proved by experience to be the most helpful for surfacing things which the student already knows about him or herself—but cannot immediately articulate.

That is true throughout this course, but never more so than in this section dealing with the autobiography, and the subsequent material based upon it: skill identification, clustering, and prioritizing of the clusters.

MOTIVATION. Explain that if insufficient time and attention is spent on this work-autobiography, it will *cripple* the effectiveness of the entire rest of the program, for that particular student. Or, to use the Mining metaphor (see the goal statements, to the left) students will

6. Then *the rationale for the Autobiography*, and some explanation of skill identification (Appendix B) so that the students can see *why* they are asked to do it.

7. *Questions from the students* concerning the rationale. (Here we see how crucial it is that the instructor shall first have done this course for his or her own life.)

8. *A practical demonstration* of *why* the Work-Autobiography needs to be thorough. It has been discovered that class members do not always understand how detailed the work-autobiography needs to be—until they get to the part of the course where the autobiography is taken and used as the basis for skill-identification. It is therefore *crucial* that, at this point, some simple practice be given to the class in skill-identification, in order that they may understand why the autobiography needs to be so detailed. The Practice is to be found in Appendix I.

It is important to emphasize, however, that skill-identification is only one of the reasons for the autobiography; and the other goals are *equally* important.

9. *A detailed explanation of the homework.* Only *after* the students have seen why the work-autobiography should be so detailed, ought you to give them the exact mechanics for ensuring that it will be detailed (opposite page). But do go into these mechanics very carefully.

student

Goal:
To make sure
that the work-
autobiography is
complete, with
no period
omitted.

Goal:
To begin to focus
your attention
on the genuine
accomplishments
you have
already brought
to pass.

Goal:
To aid you in
surfacing more
memories; getting
bad memories out
of the way some-
times then frees
good memories
to float to the
surface of your
consciousness
more.

Goal:
To help increase
your
self-confidence.

To aid you in being thorough and comprehensive, we suggest you first fill out the form
in Appendix B, of this manual.

ooooooooooooooooooooooooooooooooooooooooooooooooooooooooooooooo

Do it now, please.

ooooooooooooooooooooooooooooooooooooooooooooooooooooooooooooooo

Now, use the summary of your adult working
experience in Appendix B as *the framework*
for your detailed work-autobiography. i.e.,

Copy the first full-entry listed there. Then
try to describe just exactly what you did
there, what you accomplished (always try to
present exact numerical quantities or the
best approximation available to you. Insert
numbers, dollar figures, percentages, and
other precise facts wherever possible) and
what you enjoyed.

Overcome your natural modesty and your
natural reluctance to blow your own horn.

Don't omit anything you did just because it
bored you. Describe it, however briefly, and
say that it bored you. Feelings are welcome,
in this document you are compiling.

In fact, spend the longest time describing the
activities you enjoyed the most. In other
words, if you were enthusiastic about something you did in that particular job, or whatever, let your enthusiasm show in the amount
of time you spend describing it. This is particularly true of accomplishments.

Your own evaluation of your accomplishments is the only one that counts. We are not
particularly concerned about what others
thought about what you did; this is to be

Error to
be avoided is:
Being so overcome
with (false)
modesty, that you
feel there is very
little you have
ever done well,
and consequently
you feel you are
going to write a
very brief
autobiography.

Error:
High school or
college students
who take this
course feeling at
this point that
they have not
enough work
experience to
fill in this
exercise.

counselor

not be able to do much mining, if they only sink a two-inch shaft.

MOTIVATION. Quote Buckminster Fuller at this point: "... You do not belong to you. You belong to the universe. The significance of you will remain forever obscure to you, but you may assume you are fulfilling your significance if you apply yourself to converting all your experience to highest advantage to others."

This is what you are doing with this work-autobiography. You are assuming that the significance of You will remain forever obscure, but that you can catch a glimpse at least of some of it here; and you are assuming that you can convert your experience, so that it is of the highest advantage in the future to others *and to you.*

ADAPTATION FOR STUDENTS. You have already done work in organizations: in your family (the prime organization of our culture), perhaps in school extra-curricular organizations; in church organizations perhaps; in your own craftwork (i.e., your own organization). Describe each, what you saw as its purpose, etc. You will sharpen your

instructor

10. *Questions* from the students.

11. *Reading assignment* also: Chapter Five in Parachute. Suggest this ought to be read *before* beginning the work-autobiography.

student

THE PROGRAM ELEMENTS IN THIS FIRST
COLUMN HELP THE STUDENT IDENTIFY HIS/HER
PRIMARY **FUNCTIONAL GOAL** (WHAT)

THE PROGRAM ELEMENTS IN THIS SECOND
COLUMN HELP THE STUDENT IDENTIFY HIS/HER
PRIMARY **ORGANIZATIONAL GOAL** (WHERE)

Goal:
To surface
enough details
about each
function you
exercised, that we
can begin to see
all the skills you
used there;
and also to help
you to see the
transferability
of those skills.

Goal:
There is
a purpose for *each*
of the questions
to follow.
Thus: ‣ ‣ ‣ ‣ ‣ ‣ ‣

Goal:
[1] To set the
background and
help you recall the
stage on which
your achievements
were enacted,
since this is the
backdrop against
which your
future movements
will take place.

Goal:
[2] To move you
to think about the
organization from the
point of view of the
head of that
organization; and
thus to move the
organization into a
larger environment;

Your Life as seen through Your Eyes, not as seen through Somebody Else's Eyes.

It is crucial that you write this work-auto-biography as though you were trying to make a young child (say, five years old) understand exactly what you did. Thus you must be very detailed.

e.g., Not "I was a waitress" but: "I was responsible for waiting on ten tables at one time in this restaurant, taking orders from all the people at the table as to what they wanted to eat, then giving the orders in at the kitchen to the cooks there. I had to keep in mind who had been served with what, and keep some kind of timing schedule in my head so that I would know which table had waited the longest for its next course (of food) etc., etc."

Be sure to break down each working segment of your life into sub-components of not more than 2—3 years.

In describing *each* segment, in addition to whatever else you wish to say, please be *certain* to answer the following questions:

(1) Briefly describe the organization to which you were assigned or in which you worked, including its approximate size, general purpose or mission, anything unusual about it or its situation, and any other details which clarify the circumstances under which you worked.

(2) Briefly outline your responsibilities, numbers of personnel supervised, types and amounts of equipment items involved, and

Error:
Leaving the
mistaken impression
with anyone along
the way that you
have no experience
in money manage-
ment, never heard of
a budget, know
nothing about
economy, and have
no idea of the value
of a hard earned
dollar. So, be sure
to give all possible
details on every bit
of experience you
have had in money-
management, to
combat this
impression.

8

counselor

READ THE THIRD COLUMN ON EACH PAGE
WHEN WORKING WITH **INDIVIDUALS**

perception of 'milieu's in a way that will
stand you in excellent stead, for your
future.

EXPLANATION. The truth that no matter how
much you may dislike accounting and similar
financial work, your chances of reaching your
ultimate goal will be enhanced if you can
truthfully claim that you know something
about this subject (unless your salary, or
profits, are to be paid in wampum, lovebeads
or the like).

So, search for any experiences you have had
in:
• cost analyses, estimates and projections;
• financial planning;
• fiscal programming;
• budget planning, preparation, justification,
    administration & analysis;
• audits & fiscal controls;
   etc.

UNDERLINING. If your next job (or career) is
going to be in some kind of a group activity
or organization (and we must assume that is
what will occur in the case of the majority of
students, since experience indicates thare are
not as many 'loners' in the world of work as
we sometimes hear portrayed in the press,
and elsewhere), your only real job security,
job insurance, and personal sense of worth is

instructor

READ THE FOURTH COLUMN ON EACH PAGE
WHEN WORKING WITH **GROUPS**, WORKSHOPS, CONFERENCES, ETC.

NOT TO BE TAUGHT TO OTHERS UNTIL THE INSTRUCTOR HAS FIRST TAKEN THE COURSE HIM (HER) SELF.

9

student

compared to other organizations, what was unusual about this one and its mission?

Goal:
[3] To see something positive about each period of your life; also, to ease you out of jargon and into reality. To begin to enforce and reinforce the supremacy of your own opinions, rather than any other's, when it comes to evaluating yourself. To get you to break out of stereotypes. To get you thinking of work as people-environments and to get you thinking in these terms so that for now and for the future all job-related experiences will be seen as essentially a matter of people interactions.

Goal:
[4] To elevate your own self-esteem, the key is The Things The Supervisor Never Noticed. To reinforce the

your dollar estimates of your fund and property accountability. Without going into minute detail, explain exactly what you did while you held this position. Use your own language; do not quote from manuals. Try to avoid the jargon of your profession, whenever possible.

(3) Describe any portions of this experience which you considered significant at the time, particularly concerning your relations with others.

The magnitude or extent of the achievement is not at all important. e.g., something that saved \$2 is as important as something that saved \$2,000,000, because the principle is the same.

(4) Describe anything you did which *you* think of as either a personal contribution to the organization, or as a significant personal achievement—especially considering your age and experience at that time. Speak up, please, this is no time for false modesty!

(5) Describe achievements which went particularly well, and you didn't even have to try.

(6) Describe briefly any participation in civic, church, fraternal, sports, or *any other* after-hours activity or interest (e.g., artistic, handicraft, gardening, entrepreneurial, or whatever).

REPEAT THIS PROCEDURE, AND THESE SIX QUESTIONS, FOR EACH OF THE REMAINING SEGMENTS YOU HAVE LISTED IN APPENDIX B, UNDER YOUR ADULT WORKING-EXPERIENCE.

Treat each time segment as though it were the only one you ever had. You must devote just as much thought and attention to your early time segments, as to those in your later years.

Error:
Thinking your experience with money has been too minor to be worth mentioning.

Error:
Thinking only of achievements for which you received awards, citations, or some other honor.

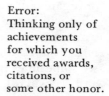

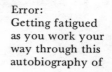

Error:
Getting fatigued as you work your way through this autobiography of

counselor

in your *outproducing* your peers all the time. You are beginning now, by looking at your achievements, to gather material for showing, from the first, what an imaginative resourceful person you are, and what an asset you would be in any organization.

ADAPTATION. Housewives have managed the household budget money. Students have managed allowances, or money made from part-time jobs, or from their own handcraftsmanship (or handcraftswomanship). How did you manage it? Did you save money anywhere? How? Did you use it as capital anywhere (say, to buy materials for your craft)? If so, what profit return did you get when that capital was put to use? You *do* know something about the management of money, and this is the place to put it in.

WIDENING MENTAL HORIZONS. In what ways would any of the organizations you have served (family, school, church, community, business, your own enterprise, etc.) have been poorer in profits, in resources, in values, etc. if you had never been there? What *did* you contribute, or what did you overcome in your

instructor

NOT TO BE TAUGHT TO OTHERS UNTIL THE INSTRUCTOR HAS FIRST TAKEN THE COURSE HIM (HER) SELF.

11

student

idea that the only record which counts for *you* is your own memory bank.

Goal:
[5] To help you dredge up your greatest strengths— your natural born talents. See explanation of Skills, p. 177. No way anyone can compete with your *natural* talents.

Goal:
[6] To get at the whole purpose of this course: *what do you do when no one else is telling you what to do?* So as to begin to free you to go do what you most want to do, rather than what people tell you you have to do. To find the inner drive, rather than the outer one.

Goal:
To warm up your communicating skills all over again, by discarding inhibiting influences.

If you are still in, or just out of, school, instead of the above questions, tell about:

a) part-time jobs;

b) extra-curricular activities, at home and on campus;

c) initiatives you showed in the family, or elsewhere.

If you have not had what the nit-pickers would call 'significant working experience', remember that whatever you were doing constructively, was in fact work of value. In such instances, break the past time into time-segments on the basis of your main interests, activities, and/or enthusiasms.

If you have had a lot of work-experience, but it was not in 'straight' organizations, but more entrepreneurial, or artistic, or outdoorsy, or whatever, then (as above) break the time past into time-segments on the basis of your interests, enthusiasms, etc.—and ignore whichever questions among the Six, above, do not seem to apply to each segment.

When you write your work-autobiography, forget the common practice of understating one's own achievements, or of being reluctant to use the pronoun "I". Use it as frequently as possible. We want you to talk about yourself. Please do so in a straightforward fashion.

Please write informally, and at length. Forget any training you may ever have had about keeping communications brief. Rather, 'ramble' as much as you want to. If you omit to give the whole picture, the only person you will hurt will be yourself.

yours, and hence putting down less detail as you come to each later work-segment.

Error:
Thinking that only what you did in the formal 'job market-place' can really count as 'work'.

Error:
Thinking of this particular program element as something inflexible and fixed, that must be used by every student—young or old, male or female, white collar or blue collar, in exactly the same way.

counselor

instructor

own life that you felt was an important achievement in your own eyes? e.g., If you had a broken stereo, and it defeated your every attempt to fix it on your own, until one day you just determined you were going to fix it no matter what, and you persisted until you were successful—that is the kind of personal triumph that belongs in your work-autobiography.

EXPLANATION. Whenever you were using your hands or your eyes or your head or your feet you were performing a *function,* and functions are but another word for "skills". What kinds of activities you engaged in, and what kinds of functions you enjoyed performing in your after-hours time may be the most significant and important discovery in this course, for you.

EXHORTATION. When you have completed each time segment, forget it, and start the next time segment as though it were the very first one that you were writing on.

FLEXIBILITY. You are free to adapt these questions so that they make sense to *you,* as long as the manner in which you adapt them does not lead to a) a very brief work-auto-biography, or b) a work-autobiography that is so general and undetailed there is no way that any skill identification can be made from it.

NOT TO BE TAUGHT TO OTHERS UNTIL THE INSTRUCTOR HAS FIRST TAKEN THE COURSE HIM (HER) SELF.

13

student

Goal:
To help self-esteem rise, as new achievements recur again and again, in each segment.

Goal:
To help you (eventually) to see Patterns through all the various segments of your life.

Goal:
To help you see this chief revealed truth:
with few exceptions if any, it hasn't mattered what organization you were in: your talents still have shown.

Goal:
To dredge up memories, and achievements.
To stimulate your memory banks.

Goal:
To show you how to go about the practical task of getting this autobiography written, in the midst of your busy and already over-crowded schedule.

Start thinking as though you were already in a new career, now looking back. As you look back, claim every bit of credit that legitimately is yours. You are responsible for what those under you achieved, if you were participant in any way: "I recognized such and such a problem, I got so and so to get to work on it, and as a result . . . " Etc. Tell us about your role: why, how and what *You* did.

If, during your writing of the work-autobiography, you recall any negative experiences along the way, a little soul-searching honesty on your part about any contribution you may have made to your own past misfortunes is usually an excellent investment, to avoid as much as possible any future repetition of such past difficulty. An ounce of prevention is worth a ton of regrets. However, do not dwell on what you did that was wrong in the past; your major thrust is to search for your achievements and positive strengths.

YOU WILL FIND IT BEST, IN WRITING THIS AUTOBIOGRAPHY, TO SET A STEADY PACE OF SO MUCH TIME PER DAY, SO MANY HOURS PER WEEK—
since recollection is best exploited by steady persistent application.

Error:
Talking only about what was going on in the environment outside of you, instead of what *you* were doing to the environment yourself.

Error:
Allowing any negative experiences you have had, to become the sum total of all that you write about in your work-autobiography.

counselor

EXPANDING HORIZONS. Look at the influence which you had on other people, when—in each time segment—you are recounting your achievements and accomplishments. "Arousing the apathetic into meaningful dialogue and action" is an example of the kind of skill you may uncover, as you think about it.

PERSPECTIVE. It is important to look at and profit from negative experiences, but only when these are viewed as a relatively minor element in the much larger context of your whole life, with all its positive (often over-looked) accomplishments. The difficulty with some so-called 'personnel experts' is that *all* they ever have a person think about are his/her negative experiences.

[Note to the instructor: since you have already taken this course for your own life, do not hesitate—at appropriate spots throughout the course—to use illustrations from your own life. This helps personalize the course, *as long as you do not talk about yourself too much*—thus turning this course into merely your own personal ego trip. It is best done in answer to students' questions.]

instructor

12. If you have any time left over, you might want to set the students to writing an excerpt from their coming autobiography—such as "a typical day in their present life"—then, if time still permits, after the excerpts are written, break into groups of threes, and discuss what skills the other two see in the third person's excerpt (as s/he reads it aloud). Go on to the next person every 5 minutes.

Experience has revealed that it is helpful beyond belief if the course can, following this first session, adjourn for two (or three) weeks, before it meets again. Three is optimum.

Indeed, it is helpful to have the criterion that students will be dropped from the course if—when the class reconvenes three weeks hence—they

NOT TO BE TAUGHT TO OTHERS UNTIL THE INSTRUCTOR HAS FIRST TAKEN THE COURSE HIM (HER) SELF.

15

student

THE PROGRAM ELEMENTS IN THIS FIRST
COLUMN HELP THE STUDENT IDENTIFY HIS/HER
PRIMARY **FUNCTIONAL GOAL** (WHAT)

THE PROGRAM ELEMENTS IN THIS SECOND
COLUMN HELP THE STUDENT IDENTIFY HIS/HER
PRIMARY **ORGANIZATIONAL GOAL** (WHERE)

instructor

READ THE FOURTH COLUMN ON EACH PAGE
WHEN WORKING WITH **GROUPS**, WORKSHOPS, CONFERENCES, ETC.

have not totally completed their work-autobiography. We stress this, because in pilot experiments, some students remained hopelessly behind throughout the entire course, just because they never completed their work-autobiography, *on which all else depends.*

SECOND CLASS SESSION
SOME SUGGESTED PROGRAM ELEMENTS

1. LOOKING BACK

a. Check on homework reading in *Parachute,* Chapter 5. It may be wise for the instructor to mention one or two important points from the reading. If desirable, a group discussion can be held on the question of which method of life-planning the class prefers: going back to the past 'for mining purposes'; dealing with feelings about the present; or indulging in future dreams. [After discussion, it may be pointed out that this course will deal with all three.]

b. Check on who completed work-autobiography, and who didn't. It is useful to go around the class and put numbers up on a blackboard or piece of newsprint, to see what the average number of pages was for everyone. If someone is hopelessly behind, and the class wants to continue him with the rest of the class, it is useful to appoint a 'buddy system' with someone who really enjoyed the exercise (ask for a show of hands to discover who they were) agreeing to meet with the slower student two or three times prior to the next class session, in order to get him or her caught up.

NOT TO BE TAUGHT TO OTHERS UNTIL THE INSTRUCTOR HAS FIRST TAKEN THE COURSE HIM (HER) SELF.

17

student

THE PROGRAM ELEMENTS IN THIS FIRST
COLUMN HELP THE STUDENT IDENTIFY HIS/HER
PRIMARY **FUNCTIONAL GOAL** (WHAT)

THE PROGRAM ELEMENTS IN THIS SECOND
COLUMN HELP THE STUDENT IDENTIFY HIS/HER
PRIMARY **ORGANIZATIONAL GOAL** (WHERE)

Goal:
To make you
review the whole
list of achievements
contained in your
autobiography,
and focus your
attention on them
as one solid string,
now minus the
setting or backdrop
against which
they occurred.

Goal:
To get you out of
your sub-culture,
and into others, by
beginning to learn
other languages;
to get you inquiring,
since mind-
broadening is
crucial; to make
you well-informed,
since the main
work of someone
worth hiring (or
someone worth
patronizing, if you
decide to go out on
your own) is
evidence that s/he
is well-informed;
to start you thinking
on a higher level.

2.A Most Important Achievements

When, and only when, your whole work-
autobiography is completed, and done
thoroughly, then
please describe briefly, in descending order
of importance (the most important, first;
the least important, last),
what *you* consider to be the Five most important achievements of your entire career
(or life), to date.

2.B Reading

We ask you to start doing some reading, on
a regular basis, in modern management literature—and even to build your own library.

You should discover for yourself what books
are most helpful *to you* for *your* purposes.
We will suggest some which *may* be of interest,
and consequently of help, to you. But you be
the judge. Never never assume that because
it is in print, it is therefore true. Many con-
tain some glaring and fatal errors, and to
follow such dubious advice is to place yourself in dreadful jeopardy.

As a rule, you will discover that books on
survival for the already-employed executive
tend to be of uniformly higher quality, than
books on job-hunting. The reason is simple,
of course: the rules for surviving once one
has a job are far better understood than the
process by which one finds meaningful and
appropriate employment for oneself.

Error:
Relying on
other people's
opinions about
what your five
most important
achievements
are, instead of
relying on your
own opinion
and judgment.

Error:
The feeling that
this all has to
be read overnight;
(it is only impor-
tant that you keep
at it, on some
regular reading
schedule.)

Error:
The assumption
that, because it
is in print, it
is therefore true.

counselor

instructor

UNDERLINING. Emphasize: Only your own opinion counts; no one else's at this point in the process. It doesn't matter if no one else even knew about the incident or accomplishment that you have in mind as one of your Five. If you get a warm glow of happiness and pride thinking about it now, it is worth considering as one of your top choices.

REQUIRED:

What Color Is Your Parachute? A Practical Manual for Job-Hunters & Career-Changers by Richard N. Bolles, (Ten Speed Press, Box 4310, Berkeley CA 94704, 1972).

SUGGESTIONS:

You, Inc. A detailed escape route to being your own boss, by Peter Weaver (Doubleday).

Business As a Game, by Albert Z. Carr (Signet Books, published by the New American Library).

Survival in the Executive Jungle, by Chester Burger (MacMillan).

The Brain Watchers, by Martin L. Gross (Random House).

Up the Organization, by Robert Townsend (Fawcett Crest, published by Fawcett Publications).

The Peter Principle, by Laurence F. Peter & Raymond Hull (William Morrow & Company, Inc).

Men, Ideas & Politics, by Peter F. Drucker (Harper & Row).

Work in America, by a Special Task Force (M.I.T. Press).

2. LOOKING AHEAD

a. Present and discuss the program element to the left: "MOST IMPORTANT ACHIEVEMENTS". This is to be done as homework before the next session. (They will need the carbon copy of their work-autobiography, to work from.)

b. Present and discuss the READING assignment, at the left.

student

THE PROGRAM ELEMENTS IN THIS FIRST
COLUMN HELP THE STUDENT IDENTIFY HIS/HER
PRIMARY **FUNCTIONAL GOAL** (WHAT)

THE PROGRAM ELEMENTS IN THIS SECOND
COLUMN HELP THE STUDENT IDENTIFY HIS/HER
PRIMARY **ORGANIZATIONAL GOAL** (WHERE)

OVERVIEW—
After a time lag
between this and
the previous
exercise, in order
to allow the
brain to cogitate,
you proceed to
this exercise,
whose goal is:
To clarify for you
how to relate your
experience to
specifics—a process
and skill which is
essential to your
ultimate identifica-
tion of your
primary functional
goal, not to
mention your
ultimate success
in 'selling yourself'
to others.

2.c A Summary of Professional Skills

Please review your work on all elements in
the preceding assignment, and identify as
many as possible of the *specific* professional,
managerial or executive skills that you have
successfully demonstrated in the past.

A sample skills list is to be found in Appendix
C. If you do not understand any of the
terms on this sample list, please look it up in
a dictionary, if necessary.

Then, using *each* skill that you have identified (in turn), go back over your work-autobiography, and write a brief summary of
exactly what you can do (because you *did*
do it) in each skill-area.

**Write down, or discuss, anything that is worrying you
about this whole process, up to this point, please.**

Error:
Vague terms,
such as
"administration",
"sales",
"production", etc.
To avoid this,
describe what
type of sales, or
administration,
etc.

Goal:
To get you to talk
about what you
think the whole
world of the job-
hunt is like, out
there; and to
identify what
frightens you
about it.

3. Hampering Factors for Your Job-Hunt

Disregarding any presumed disadvantages of
your background *for the task of job-hunting,*
describe any personality or other factors
which you feel may hamper you in your job
search.

Error: Thinking that
because they fear it,
it is therefore true,
i.e. if your fear is
that you cannot get
a decent job because
you are too old (too
young, too experi-
enced, too inexperi-
enced, female, or
whatever), thinking
that your fear will
become an absolute
fact.
(Bah, humbug!)

counselor

instructor

REASSURANCE. Nobody (each student needs to be told) is very good at this, at this stage. But it doesn't matter, really, because you can't help but begin to learn what we're trying to teach you: a whole new way of looking at Everything, especially Yourself.

c. Present the program element: A SUMMARY OF PROFESSIONAL SKILLS, *together with the rationale* in Appendix C. Open up for discussion. This is to be done as homework before the next class meeting.

N.B. If preferred, the instructor may at the same time introduce *the whole subject* of skill-identification, as found on page 66, and in Appendix I, here at this point. This is particularly appropriate with people who are already managers or in some position of management level.

With younger students, however, (as, in college) it is useful to have them just deal with A SUMMARY OF PROFESSIONAL SKILLS program element at this point, and not at great length, in order to learn quickly that they do indeed possess professional skills.

Then, whatever choices they later make about which skills they prefer to use, will at least be made out of a genuine sense of alternatives—and hence, freedom. "I can do other things, but this is what I prefer."

ALLAYING THEIR FEARS, AND TEACHING THEM ABOUT THE NATURE OF THE JOB-HUNT.
1. So far as each student's worries are concerned, agree with those *if you go through the traditional employment System.* Therefore, teach each student: don't have anything to do with that system. There *is* another way.

2. Instantly allay each student's worst fears by showing her/him that's not the way the

d. Present the program element: HAMPERING FACTORS FOR YOUR JOB-HUNT. This will be both homework and classroom work.

The instructor may wish to give the class a brief lecture at this point, out of his/her own experience on "The Job-Hunting System", dealing with the following points: a) What propaganda says it is
　　　　　　　　　　　　　　　 b) What it really is
　　　　　　　　　　　　　　　 c) How you go about beating it

[Resources to help you with this: Chapters Two and Three, in *Parachute*; also, for those who wish to have this explained on videotape by John Crystal himself, contact him at 6825 Redmond Drive, McLean, Virginia 22101.]

student

THE PROGRAM ELEMENTS IN THIS FIRST
COLUMN HELP THE STUDENT IDENTIFY HIS/HER
PRIMARY **FUNCTIONAL GOAL** (WHAT)

THE PROGRAM ELEMENTS IN THIS SECOND
COLUMN HELP THE STUDENT IDENTIFY HIS/HER
PRIMARY **ORGANIZATIONAL GOAL** (WHERE)

Goal:
To show how
to apply this
program element
to Anyone,
regardless of age,
sex, work experience,
personal history,
presumed handicaps
in 'the job market'
etc.

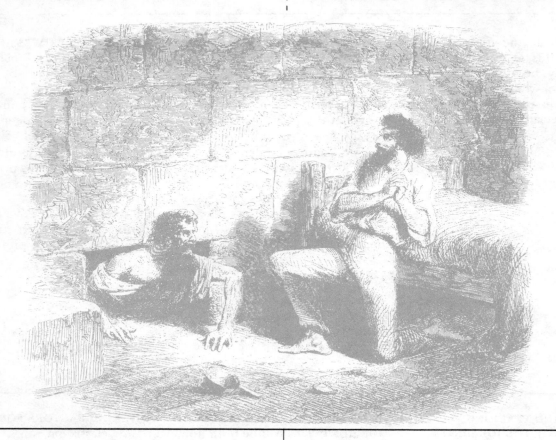

Error:
Listening to too
many horror
stories from other
people (or the
media) that
supposedly
demonstrate
incontrovertibly
that these are
fatal barriers to
getting a job.
(They are, only
IF you go about
the job-hunt the
traditional way,
which we will
show you
how to avoid
altogether.)

Goal:
To begin exploring
what you really
want to accomplish
with your life, not by
asking 'what do you
want'—but by start-
ing with the easier-to-
answer question:
'what don't you want?'

4.A Distasteful Living/ Working Conditions

Describe any living or working conditions
that you think you and/or your family
would find distasteful. Describe at length,
if necessary.

See Appendix D at this point.

counselor

job-hunt goes *if you know what you're doing, and if you know how to handle yourself.*

Specific worries you will encounter (probably) again and again:
   a. Age (too young or too old—they feel)
   b. Sex (female, particularly)
   c. Color
   d. Education (too little or too much)
   e. Experience (too little or 'overqualified')
   f. Personal things (height, posture, voice, mannerisms, etc.)
   g. Psychiatric history (if there is one)

[How you treat this last one, is indicative of how you treat the other worries:
(1) It's nobody's business if you have such a history.
(2) If you're in a process that requires you to come clean about this, you're doing it wrong.
(3) If anyone ever asks you if you have any such history, ask him if he has a form certifying *he* is OK?

There is, however, another way to go about the job-hunt: the way we are teaching in this course. And, if you go about it *that* way, all that matters is *what you are today.*]

instructor

e. Present the program element DISTASTEFUL LIVING/WORKING CONDITIONS, *plus the rationale for it*, as found in Appendix D. Discussion. This is to be a homework assignment before the next class meeting.

3. **CLASSROOM WORK**

   a. Divide the class into small groups (5—8 members) and have them discuss "Distasteful Living/Working Conditions" that they have known in their own past experience, or that they have picked up as part of their own personal agenda out of the experiences of others (parents, friends, movies, TV, books, magazine articles, newspaper articles, etc.) Use newsprint in each group, with convener and also a scribe, to put down the various conditions under which each group member does *not* want to have to live or work, if s/he can help it. (It is not necessary to have consensus before putting down a comment on the newsprint sheet; it is sufficient *if even one* member of the group feels that way about something.) If comments are repeated, put a check-mark after each, for each time it is repeated by someone else in the group. That way, the most common factors will be readily apparent.

   When the small groups reconvene in one large class, have each group report what it said.

   b. And/or: Repeat small groups, using as the topic: things which I think might be a disadvantage to me in conducting my own job-search.

   This can also be dealt with in the large class, if desired, as an alternative methodology, as long as care is taken to see that one or two people do not do all the talking.

   c. And/or: you can break up the class into trios (groups of three people) and have them do a little practice in skill-identification, using Appendix I, Section III.

These classroom exercises can be *interspersed* with the instructor's presentations, and homework explanations, if desired.

student

THE PROGRAM ELEMENTS IN THIS FIRST COLUMN HELP THE STUDENT IDENTIFY HIS/HER PRIMARY **FUNCTIONAL GOAL** (WHAT)

THE PROGRAM ELEMENTS IN THIS SECOND COLUMN HELP THE STUDENT IDENTIFY HIS/HER PRIMARY **ORGANIZATIONAL GOAL** (WHERE)

field trip, a trip away from the classroom to permit the gathering of data at first hand.

sur·vey (sẽr-vā'; *for n., usually* sũr'vā), *v.t.* [ME. *sur-veien;* Anglo-Fr. *survier,* OFr. *surveoir; sur-* (< L. *super*), over + *veoir* < L. *videre,* to see], 1. to examine for some specific purpose; inspect or consider carefully; review in detail. 2. to look at or consider, especially in a general or comprehensive way; view. 3. to determine the location, form, or boundaries of (a tract of land) by measuring the lines and angles in accordance with the principles of geometry and trigonometry. *v.i.* to survey land. *n.* [*pl.* SURVEYS (-vāz, -vāz')], 1. a general study or inspection: as, the *survey* showed a critical

counselor

READ THE THIRD COLUMN ON EACH PAGE
WHEN WORKING WITH **INDIVIDUALS**

instructor

READ THE FOURTH COLUMN ON EACH PAGE
WHEN WORKING WITH **GROUPS**, WORKSHOPS, CONFERENCES, ETC.

THIRD CLASS SESSION
SOME SUGGESTED PROGRAM ELEMENTS

1. LOOKING BACK

a. Check on who did, and who did not, do the homework exercises of last time, by a show of hands, viz.,

    MOST IMPORTANT ACHIEVEMENTS
    PROFESSIONAL SKILLS SUMMARY
    HAMPERING FACTORS FOR YOUR JOB-HUNT
    DISTASTEFUL LIVING/WORKING CONDITIONS

b. Ask what learnings they got from doing that homework. Class discussion.

c. Ask what worries them about the course to this point. Deal with those worries.

d. The instructor should make some positive response of his/her own to the student's worries, hampering factors in the job-hunt, etc., along the lines of A Guide: Analyzing a Student's Dislikes, p. 186. In other words, don't just let their worries 'lie there', but deal with them NOW.

e. With any students who did not complete all of the homework, it may be necessary for you again to adopt 'the buddy system' and appoint one of the faster students to work with one of the slower students, between now and the next class session. *It is crucial to keep the whole class together, in this course.* Since the course is experiential, not merely a head-trip, no one else can do for a student (least of all the instructor) what the student can only do for him/herself.

f. Discuss any worries about skill identification that the class may have. Go back over the material on skill-identification if necessary. Use material from the homework of the 'faster' students to illustrate (assuming they shared it with you before the class began).

Third Class Session

NOT TO BE TAUGHT TO OTHERS UNTIL THE INSTRUCTOR HAS FIRST TAKEN THE COURSE HIM (HER) SELF.

25

student

THE PROGRAM ELEMENTS IN THIS FIRST
COLUMN HELP THE STUDENT IDENTIFY HIS/HER
PRIMARY **FUNCTIONAL GOAL** (WHAT)

THE PROGRAM ELEMENTS IN THIS SECOND
COLUMN HELP THE STUDENT IDENTIFY HIS/HER
PRIMARY **ORGANIZATIONAL GOAL** (WHERE)

Goal:
To return to the
theme of
'Who Am I?'
(after the interlude
of the previous
two elements),
and to look at
an earlier segment
of your life
through different
glasses now,
looking for early
signs of *Patterns—*
on the theory
that the boy casts
the shadow of
the man (or: the
girl casts the shadow
of the woman).

4.B Educational Background

Discuss your educational background, please
(high school/college, if attended/graduate
school, if attended); and particularly:

a. The teachers you liked the best. The least.
   And, why?

b. The subjects you enjoyed the most. The
   least. *And, why?*

c. The subjects in which you made the best
   grades, or did the best. The ones in which
   you did (or feel you did) the poorest.
   And why?

Also describe briefly and comment on any
extra-curricular activities in school that might
be of even minor significance in terms of
some possible aspect of your future.

Goal:
To begin to move you
from reviewing the
Past, to preparing for
The Future somewhat
more directly now,
but *in the light of* all
that you have already
learned in this course
thus far...and there-
fore with you in a
position to be more
positive, more analyti-
cal, less fearful, and
with greater clarity
about what you really
want—at this point.

4.c Starting Over Again

In the light of your present knowledge and
experience, if you could go back and start
your education and career all over again,

what would you do differently?
and why?

[*May* be omitted if you are still in school.]

Avoid:
Hopelessness;
the feeling that
for whatever reason
(background, age,
etc.) it is just too
late to start over
again; so, why even
waste breath on
thinking about it?

counselor

instructor

[**PRACTICAL DIRECTIONS.** Needless to say, if the student taking this course is a high school or college student, this section should be given a lot of attention, time, and effort. That is to say, much 'mining' of this may have to be done, in the absence of any long work-history elsewhere. It is amazing, however, the amount of insight a student can obtain from this program element.]

2. LOOKING AHEAD

a. Present the program element EDUCATIONAL BACKGROUND for homework assignment, to be done before the next class.

INTERPRETATION AND THE ENCOURAGEMENT OF HOPE. [After the student has said what s/he would do differently, there are four points to include in your response:]
(1) Agreement and support. Great ideas! You are absolutely right.
(2) Sharing. Give your own experience where it offers support for the student's.
(3) Interpretation. "You *are* in fact starting all over *in other ways.*

b. Present the program element STARTING OVER AGAIN, as homework also. You may want to ask for a few off-the-top-of-the-head responses, so that you can answer as in the column immediately to the left.

student

Goal:
[1] To ratify all that has been uncovered thus far about your-self; and
[2] To open your eyes to new insights about your self and your work, by focusing down on a single Day and making yourself examine it; and
[3] To surface routine talents that you may have overlooked; as well as
[4] To see more significance in whatever you're doing.

4.D A Typical Working Day

In brief outline form write an account or log (preferably detailed) of what *you* regard as a typical day in your working life, in your present or last position. Describe it in as much detail as you would to a five year old child, please.

Then list the skills you see yourself as having used in that typical day,
plus your reactions to people, as well as identifying the duties you found/find distasteful.

Try to look at all of this through the eyes of a child, so that the things you perhaps have come to take for granted, may be recharged with elemental wonder.

Avoid:
Getting locked into shorthand. (In the example to the right, "doctor" is *shorthand* for the longer phrase "I wanted to contribute, etc.") In our culture we've used shorthand so long, we've forgotten what the shorthand is all about.

5. Practice Field Survey

The next program element is going to ask you: if you had a perfectly free choice, no financial worries now or for the future, and knew for a fact that you could get any job you might want, *anywhere,* which specific community in the world would you pick as your permanent home?

(At least for planning purposes at this stage, your geographical preference and your job preference must be treated as two separate questions.)

And then, we are going to ask you to make yourself the most knowledgeable person in

counselor

READ THE THIRD COLUMN ON EACH PAGE
WHEN WORKING WITH **INDIVIDUALS**

instructor

READ THE FOURTH COLUMN ON EACH PAGE
WHEN WORKING WITH **GROUPS**, WORKSHOPS, CONFERENCES, ETC.

(4) Encouragement. "Get back to your original dream for your life. What *was* your original dream?" *State it in more general terms.* e.g., "I wanted to be a doctor", may now sound impossible; but it can (and should) be restated in more general terms (whereupon it *does* become possible): "I wanted to contribute to the physical (and spiritual) well-being of people, by means of that activity which we call Medicine." Etc., etc.
[The response to this that is most called-for, is "Why not?"]

c. Present for homework the program element A TYPICAL WORKING DAY. If any student is not at present working, have him/her recall the last time they had a job, and describe a typical day at that time.

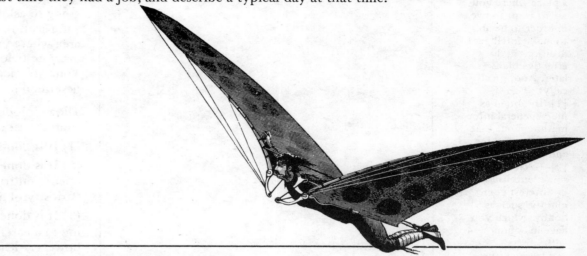

ʾ d. Present the program element PRACTICE FIELD SURVEY. *This is the heart of this particular session, and its main agenda.* We suggest you present this program element in a very special way, as follows:

(1) Present to the class the introductory material concerning the PRACTICE FIELD SURVEY (in the 'Program Element' column, down to the dotted line).

(2) Then, present the rationale for the Practice Field Survey and the Geographical Preference choice, Appendix E.

(3) In order to get the class into the frame of mind at this point, have them think out their experiences with all the places they have lived thus far. It is useful to break the class into small groups (6—8 members) and have them discuss the places they have lived, in order to elicit the factors they liked and the factors they disliked, at this point. Page 190 describes in detail how this exercise may be carried out.

(4) Point out that in the next session they are going to be asked to start thinking, in view of these factors, what city or community (anywhere in the world) they would most like to live in; but for the time

Goal:
To see *how* to learn
everything you
need to know about
a place where you
might want to live,
in order to be able
to make intelligent
decisions and
effective plans
later. And, specifi-
cally:
[1] To obtain as
much general infor-
mation about that
town as possible;
and
[2] To choose
some 'enthusiasm'
or 'interest com-
munity' such as a
hobby, which you
have in common
with others—
and learn all there
is to know about
those others in
that town who
share your interest,
including everybody
of any standing
in that town.

student

the country on the economy of your chosen
area (or areas) and learn how to conduct an
on-site personal survey of the ground you
have selected. *In preparation* for this, we are
going to ask you *now* to choose a community
(or a section of a community) in the general
area where you presently live, and do a
practice field survey of that community.
Your practice survey methodology is
described in Appendix E.

The methodology has three principal
characteristics:

(1) It is "on-site".

(2) It is done with your eyes & ears wide
open; you try to look at everything with the
curiosity of a small child.

(3) It is done by talking with people, according to a careful well-thought-out plan; which—
however—leaves room for improvisation,
serendipity, and the chance encounter.

● ●

It is important to do your homework or
preparation well, before you go out on the
practice survey, 'in the field'.

Pretend that whatever community or town
you have chosen *for your practice* really is
your own personal Shangri-La, where you
would most prefer to live in all the world.
What information would you need to know,
in order to discover if in truth you would
want to settle there?

Avoid:
Feeling this
exercise is going
to be senseless,
because you are
'going to have
to go where
the jobs are'.

counselor

DOES IT WORK? There is, indeed, no guarantee that you will find just exactly what you want, where you want it. But it is amazing in the fifteen year history of this course, how many students have ended up doing exactly that.

There are two reasons:

(1) The nature of the job-market. There are lots of 'hidden' jobs in every town, if only you know how to find them, and how to recognize them when you find them. This course will teach you precisely that. But such knowledge will only benefit you if you *first* do the work of surfacing what is going on inside your heart and head; because the agenda for your life has got to come from you, and no one else.

(2) The strength of the dream. Most people fail to find what they want in life for a very simple reason: they have cut down their original dream to one-eighth of its original size and strength; hence they are only hunting for one-eighth of their original dream— with only one-eighth of their heart (or gut). If you can recover your whole dream—what you really want to do with your life more than anything else, you will inevitably begin to hunt for that whole vision with all of your heart (or gut). And how much you want something *does* affect whether or not you find it.

instructor

being, the whole class is going to go out and survey—for practice—either the community in which the class is presently meeting, or some other nearby town or city on which the class might agree. As a class, then, agree on the community or city which is to be used for this practice. If the members of the class come from widely separated geographical areas, two cities can be chosen, with the class dividing up.

(5) Now, pose for them the question: "*How* would you survey a community (this or any other one) *for your own interest?*" Present at this point the remainder of the material on PRACTICE FIELD SURVEY in the "Program Element" column, so the class will understand what is meant by "your own interest". Let members of the class suggest what enthusiasm, off the top of their head, they would be interested in exploring during this practice field survey.

Divide the class into small groups of 5–8 and have them discuss the question ("*How* would you survey etc."). Alternatively, this can be done by the class as a whole. In any event, the results should be posted on large sheets of newsprint, up at the front of the class, and discussed.

(6) Then (and only then) present the remainder of the material in Appendix E, I.B—III.B. (Do not cover III.C, at this point, yet.)

student

Goal:
To acquire beginning skills in investigation.
To acquire beginning skills in interviewing (and therefore, in being interviewed).
To discover how easy it is to meet anybody you want to meet (without a resume) so long as you're honest about sharing an interest with someone.
To convince yourself how truly interesting you are found to be, when you are talking about what truly interests you.
To discover you need more information about yourself, before you do this for real.

student

A homework exercise designed to uncover these factors before you go, is to be found in Appendix E, I.A, in the back of this manual.

□□

We ask you to use it now.

□□

Then we want you to choose your strongest personal interest—whatever it is. It may, or may not have anything to do with your avocational interests, such as your hobbies. People do tend to use their spare time to do the things they really want to do. But your strongest interest may lie elsewhere. The test is how much *enthusiasm* you have for it. And since you cannot 'fake' enthusiasm, we ask you to choose the interest for which you have the greatest enthusiasm.

When you do your Practice Field Survey, we ask you to explore this Strongest Interest of yours, according to the suggestions which are to be found in Appendix E.

□□

Now, please do the Practice Survey.

□□

Avoid:
Coming across in your interviews of people 'on-site' as one who is looking for a job.

Avoid:
Being flustered if a job offer should arise, unexpectedly.

counselor

READ THE THIRD COLUMN ON EACH PAGE
WHEN WORKING WITH **INDIVIDUALS**

UNDERLINING. You are trying to learn everything you need to know in order to be able to make intelligent decisions about your life, and effective plans *later*. Do not hesitate to explain this to those *you* choose to interview, on-site.

Job offers may result anyway. If so, play it cool. You are:
(1) Pleased
(2) Interested
(3) Going to consider it when the time for such decisions comes.
(4) Will definitely keep in touch, to let him/her know how your survey progresses.

Then, *do* keep in touch. Give him/her further opportunities to see for him/herself just how bright, and extraordinarily thorough, you are.

instructor

READ THE FOURTH COLUMN ON EACH PAGE
WHEN WORKING WITH **GROUPS**, WORKSHOPS, CONFERENCES, ETC.

(7) Set a date (preferably before the next class session) for the Practice Field Survey, and if more than one community is to be used, divide the class (right now) up into teams, according to who is going to tackle which community. Be sure each class member has also chosen his/her major enthusiasm; and if anyone is puzzled as to who to go see regarding his/her enthusiasm, let the class make suggestions—at this point.

3. **CLASSROOM WORK**

a) As described above.

b) Also, if you got the students into full-fledged skill identification (Appendix I) previously, you may want to use any spare time in this session to break the class into trios, and work further on analyzing their autobiography.

FOURTH CLASS SESSION
SOME SUGGESTED PROGRAM ELEMENTS

1. **LOOKING BACK**

a. Assuming the Practice Field Survey was completed prior to this class session, have the students report in on what occurred. [If they did not complete it, then save this program element for the next class.] If, by any chance, the class is too large for much meaningful report-back, have about five or ten minutes of comments in the large class, and then break them up into groups of 5—8 members and allow them sufficient time to share with each other their experiences. Question to be dealt with, in the small groups:

Fourth Class Session

student

THE PROGRAM ELEMENTS IN THIS FIRST COLUMN HELP THE STUDENT IDENTIFY HIS/HER PRIMARY **FUNCTIONAL GOAL** (WHAT)

THE PROGRAM ELEMENTS IN THIS SECOND COLUMN HELP THE STUDENT IDENTIFY HIS/HER PRIMARY **ORGANIZATIONAL GOAL** (WHERE)

a·chieve (ə-chēv'), v.t. [ACHIEVED (-chēvd'), ACHIEVING], [ME. acheven; OFr. achever, to finish < a-, to + chief, end, head < L. caput, the head], 1. to do; do successfully; accomplish. 2. to get or reach by exertion; attain; gain. v.i. to effect a desired end; see perform, reach.

a·chieve·ment (ə-chēv'mənt), n. [see ACHIEVE]. 1. an achieving. 2. a thing achieved, especially by skill, work, courage, etc.

bunch (bunch), n. [ME. bunche, bonch, a hump; akin to MLG. bunk, D. bonk, Norw. bunka, a hump, heap, bunch]; 1. a cluster or tuft of things growing together; as, a bunch of grapes. 2. a collection of things of the same kind fastened or grouped together, or regarded as belonging together; as, a bunch of keys. Abbreviated bch. 3. [Rare], a hump. 4. [Colloq.], a group (of people). v.t. & v.i. 1. to form or collect into a bunch

ca·reer (kə-rēr'), n. [Early Mod. Eng. careere, carreer; Fr. carrière, road, racecourse; It. carriera < carro; see CAR]. 1. originally, a racing course; hence, 2. a swift course, as of the sun through the sky; hence, 3. full speed. 4. one's progress through life. 5. one's advancement or achievement in a particular vocation; hence, 6. a lifework; profession; occupation.

clus·ter (klus'tēr), n. [ME.; AS. clyster, cluster (akin to north G. dial. kluster) with clys-, clus- for Gmc. *klut, base of clot], 1. a number of things of the same sort gathered together or growing together; bunch. 2. a number of persons, animals, or things grouped together. v.i. & v.t. to gather or grow in a cluster or clusters.

field trip, a trip away from the classroom to permit the gathering of data at first hand.

i·den·ti·fy (ī-den'tə-fī'), v.t. [IDENTIFIED (-fīd'), IDENTIFYING], [ML. *identificare; see IDENTICAL & -FY], 1. to make identical; consider or treat as the same: as, identify your interests with ours. 2. to show to be a certain person or thing; fix the identity of; show to be the same as something or someone assumed, described, or claimed. 3. to join or associate closely; as, he has become identified with the labor movement. 4. in psychoanalysis, to make identification of (oneself) with someone else; often used absolutely.

job (job), n. [ME. gobbe, a lump, portion; orig., mouthful < Celt. gob, gop, the mouth], 1. a piece of work; definite piece of work, as in one's trade, or done by agreement for pay. 2. anything one has to do; task; chore; duty. 3. the thing or material being worked on. 4. a thing done supposedly in the public interest but actually for private gain; dishonest piece of official business. 5. a position of employment; situation; work. 6. [Colloq.], a criminal act or deed, as a theft, etc. 7. [Colloq.], any happening, affair, etc. adj. hired or done by the job; see also job lot.

plan (plan), n. [Fr. plan, earlier also plant; It. pianta (< L. planta, sole of the foot) or piano (< L. planus, plane, level)], 1. an outline; draft; map. 2. a drawing or diagram showing the arrangement in horizontal section of a structure, piece of ground, etc. 3. a scheme for making, doing, or arranging something; project; program; schedule. 4. in perspective, one of several planes thought of as perpendicular to the line of sight and between the eye and the object. v.t. [PLANNED (pland), PLANNING], 1. to make a plan of (a structure,

pro·pos·al (prə-pō'z'l), n. 1. a proposing. 2. a plan, scheme, etc. proposed. 3. an offer of marriage.
SYN.—proposal refers to a plan, offer, etc. presented for acceptance or rejection (his proposal for a decrease in taxes was approved); proposition, commonly used in place of proposal with reference to business dealings and the like, in a strict sense implies a statement, theorem, etc. set forth for discussion.

skill (skil), n. [ME., discernment, reason; ON. skil, distinction, etc.; akin to skilja, to cut apart, separate, etc.; IE. base *sqel-, to cut (cf. SHIELD, SHILLING); basic sense "ability to separate," hence "discernment"], 1. great ability or proficiency; expertness: as, his skill in mathematics is well known. 2. an art, craft, or science, especially one involving the use of the hands or body; hence, 3. ability in such an art, craft, or science. 4. [Obs.], knowledge; understanding; judgment. v.i. [Archaic], to matter, avail, or make a difference; as, what skills it that we suffer? —SYN. see art.

spec·i·fi·ca·tion (spes'ə-fi-kā'shən), n. [ML. specificatio], 1. a specifying; detailed mention or definition. 2. usually pl. a detailed description of the parts of a whole; statement or enumeration of particulars, as to size,

con·tact (kon'takt), n. [L. contactus, pp. of contingere, to touch, seize < com-, together + tangere, to touch < IE. base *tag-, to touch; hence akin to Goth. tekan, to touch, AS. thaccian, to pat, stroke gently], 1. the act of touching or meeting: as, some shells explode only by contact with other objects. 2. the state of being in touch or association (with): as, you will come into contact with many new ideas. 3. connection: as, he made some valuable contacts at the convention, the pilot of the airplane tried to make contact with his base. 4. in electricity, a) a connection or point of connection between two conductors in a circuit. b) a device for making such a connection. v.t. 1. to place in contact. 2. to come into contact with; get in touch with: now widely used in this sense despite objections. v.i. to be in contact; come into contact. interj. ready!: a signal in aviation that everything is set for the engine to be started.

survival of the fittest, see natural selection.

sur·vive (sēr-vīv'), v.t. [SURVIVED (-vīvd'), SURVIVING], [ME. surviven; OFr. survivre; L. supervivere; super-, above + vivere, to live], 1. to live or exist longer than or beyond the life or existence of; outlive. 2. to continue to live after or in spite of; as, we survived the wreck. v.i. to continue living or existing, as after an event or after another's death. —SYN. see outlive.

tar·get (tär'git), n. [ME.; OFr. targette, dim. of targe, a shield; see TARGE]. 1. originally, a small shield, especially a round one. 2. a round, flat, e. o something resembling a target in shape or use, as the sliding sight on a surveyor's leveling rod, a disk-shaped signal on a railroad switch, the metallic surface (in an X-ray tube) upon which the stream of cathode rays impinge and from which X rays emanate, etc. Abbreviated t.

au·to·bi·og·ra·phy (ô'tə-bī-og'rə-fi, ô'tō-bi-og'rə-fi), n. [pl. AUTOBIOGRAPHIES (-fiz)], [auto- + bio- + -graphy]. 1. the art or practice of writing the story of one's own life. 2. the story of one's own life written by oneself.

work (wûrk), n. [ME. werk; AS. werc, weorc; akin to werk; IE. base *werg-, to do, act, seen also in Gr. (for *wergon), action, work (cf. ERG), organon, instrument (cf. ORGAN)], 1. bodily or mental effort exerted to do or make something; purposeful activity; labor; toil. 2. employment: as, out of work. 3. occupation; business; trade; craft; profession: as, his work. 4. something one is making, doing, or accomplishing; specifically, a) one's occupation or duty; undertaking: as, he laid out his work. b) the amount of this: as, a day's work. 5. something that has been made or done; result of effort or activity; specifically, usually pl. an act; deed: as, a person of good works. b) pl. collected writings: as, the works of Whittier. c) pl. engineering structures, as bridges, dams, etc. d) a fortification. e) needlework; embroidery; work of art. 6. material that is being or is to be processed, as in a machine tool, in some stage of manufacture. 7. pl. [construed as sing.], a place where work is done, as a factory, public utility plant, etc. 8. the working parts of a watch, etc.; mechanism. 9. manner, style, quality, rate, etc. of working; workmanship. 10. foam due to fermentation, as in cider. 11. in mechanics, transference of force from one body or system to another, measured by the product of the force and the amount of displacement in the line of force. 12. pl. in theology, moral acts; distinguished from faith. Abbreviated W., w. adj. of, for, or used in work. v.t. [WORKED (wûrkt) or WROUGHT (rôt), WORKING], wyrcan, wircan, wercan], 1. to exert oneself in order to do or make something; do work; labor; toil. 2. to be employed. 3. to perform its function; operate. 4. to ferment. 5. to operate effectively; be effectual: as, the makeshift works. 6. to produce results or exert an influence; as, let it work in their minds. 7. to be moved, manipulated, kneaded, etc. as, this putty works easily; move, proceed, etc. slowly and with or as with difficulty. 9. to move, twitch, etc. as from agitation: as, his face worked with emotion. 10. to change into a specified condition, as by repeated movement: as, the screw worked loose. 11. to make a passage: as, her elbow worked through her sleeve. 12. in nautical usage, to strain so, as in a storm, that the fastenings become slack: said of a ship. v.t. 1. to cause; bring about; effect: as, his idea worked harm. 2. to mold; shape; form: as, she works silver. 3. to weave, knit, embroider, etc.: as, she worked the sweater. 4. to solve (a mathematical problem). 5. to draw, paint, carve, etc. (a portrait or likeness). 6. to manipulate; knead: as, work the butter well. 7. to bring into a specified condition, as by repeated movement: as, they worked it loose. 8. to cultivate (soil). 9. to cause to function; operate; manage; use. 10. to cause to ferment. 11. to cause to work: as, he works his men hard. 12. to influence; persuade; induce: as, work him to your way of thinking. 13. to make (one's way), passage, etc. by work or effort. 14. to provoke; rouse: as, she worked herself into a rage. 15. to carry on activity in; operate in; cover: as, the salesman who works this region. 16. [Colloq.], to make use of, especially by contriving: as, work your connections. 17. [Colloq.], to use artifice with (a person) to gain some personal advantage.

counselor

READ THE THIRD COLUMN ON EACH PAGE
WHEN WORKING WITH **INDIVIDUALS**

instructor

READ THE FOURTH COLUMN ON EACH PAGE
WHEN WORKING WITH **GROUPS**, WORKSHOPS, CONFERENCES, ETC.

(1) What did you enjoy the most about the experience?

(2) What did you learn?

(3) What do you feel you still need to know (what puzzles you) before you go out to do this 'for real'?

When the whole class is back together, have each group report in. The instructor should encourage the class itself to try to answer the questions which still puzzle anyone *about the process, and how you gather information.* Following this:

the class should be encouraged to re-read Appendix E, I.B.—III.B.

any questions still unanswered should be left to *"the actual survey"*. Experience itself may yield the answer.

b. Discuss the homework assignments from last time, viz.,

EDUCATIONAL BACKGROUND
STARTING OVER AGAIN
A TYPICAL WORKING DAY

Ask for a show of hands as to how many did all the exercises. If any sizeable proportion of the class is behind, ask for reasons (there may be something going on that you need to pay attention to). Also, you may want to pair some of those who have completed all assignments with those who are slower, to work together in the interval between now and the next class session.

If so, do it now.

c. Ask what learnings they received from the exercises. Whole class discussion.

d. Ask what they have learned about themselves, from the exercises.

e. Check also how they've been doing with the reading (*Parachute,* management literature, the world of work, etc.). What learnings stand out in their mind, so far, from what they've read? Have whole class discussion, of this.

6. Your Geographical Preference

If you had a perfectly free choice, no financial worries, and knew for a fact that you could find the work you most wanted to do *anywhere* you chose,

1. Which specific community—town or city—would you pick as your permanent home? Consider the factors from your past experience that are important to you (Appendix E, I.A.1.2.&3.).

2. List the factors which have led you to choose that community.

3. If something unforeseen intervened to block you from your first choice, which community would you pick in this country (or elsewhere) as your second choice? And: because of *which* factors?

4. Which community would be your third choice? Factors important to that choice?

Goal:
[1] To reduce the problem of "where?" to maneageable proportions.
[2] To ensure that you consider all pertinent factors, including the possibility that your old unexamined dreams have changed.
[3] To avoid your being locked into just one possibility.
[4] To always have more than one alternative for your geographical search.

Avoid:
Confusing the issue by trying to be 'realistic' about your preference. We shall worry about ways and means later; for now: dare to dream.

7. Starting Your Contacts List

Experience shows that for most students the single best source of vital information and direct leads, later on in this process, has been their own circle of friends and acquaintances. (See *Rationale*, on page 197.)

But, *now* and not *then* is the time to start compiling that list of Contacts.

To begin with, you must cast as broad a net as possible. *No one* who would even remem-

Goal:
To get you started on building a network that includes *everyone* with whom you had/ have even a smiling relationship.

counselor

READ THE THIRD COLUMN ON EACH PAGE
WHEN WORKING WITH **INDIVIDUALS**

instructor

READ THE FOURTH COLUMN ON EACH PAGE
WHEN WORKING WITH **GROUPS**, WORKSHOPS, CONFERENCES, ETC.

PRACTICAL SUGGESTION. You may want to construct a chart (if you have an orderly mind, and want a methodical way for going about selecting your geographical preference.) This is especially true if there are two or more communities that you feel might interest you equally. List the factors that interest *you* across the top, the names of the communities down the side; check off, and then compare; e.g.,

	Clean Air	Low Crime	Warm Climate	Etc.
Boise				
L.A.				
Denver				
Miami				

2. LOOKING AHEAD

a. Present the program element YOUR GEOGRAPHICAL PREFERENCE for homework assignment, to be done before the next class.

b. Present the program element STARTING YOUR CONTACTS LIST for homework assignment, together with the rationale on page 197. Have class questions and discussion, then. Let the class answer the questions wherever possible ("Anyone have any ideas about this?" "Anyone have any idea how to help _____ with that one?") rather than the instructor "fielding" every one. It is, however, perfectly appropriate for the instructor to step in when no one else has any idea.

student

ber your name is to be left off your full and complete list. Later on, you may discard names if you care to; but for now, include *everybody*.

Buy some file folders, please. Also some 3 x 5″ index cards, and a cardfile to keep them in (at your 5 and 10, stationery store, or wherever).

Start a file folder labeled *"Contacts."* Start *now,* compiling the lists that are to go in that file folder.

You may prefer to use three by five cards, and a cardfile. This is your life, and this project (including what use you put it to) is under *your* control all the way.

Suggestions as to how to build the lists are under "Rationale," in Appendix F.

For each name on your list, put down:
    name
    address
    phone number
    note on how s/he can assist you
    note on how you should approach her/him.

Your assignment: to have 200 names on your Contacts list, within one week.

Then, deliberately set out to meet *new* people who share your interests—most especially in your favorite community where

Goal:
To deliberately expand your circle of contacts.
To learn, by experience, how to tap discreetly into networks— without imposing on anyone.
To find out the world regards you as a fine and interesting person, and enjoys the pleasure of meeting you—particularly when you are enthusiastic about your interests.

Avoid:
The feeling that it is somehow immoral to think of your acquaintances in terms of how they can be helpful to you. Recoiling at the thought of 'begging my friends to find me a job'; or even 'telling my friends I'm looking'.

Avoid:
Beating yourself, as you begin to list names, for not having kept in better touch with your friends, over the years.

Feeling that 'important people' are the only ones worth listing.

Not building a complete enough list.

When you meet new contacts, coming across as 'a job-hunter'.